Let's Have Fun Outside!

LET'S GO STRAWBERRY PICKING

By Kristen Rajczak Nelson

Gareth Stevens
PUBLISHING

Please visit our website, www.garethstevens.com. For a free color catalog of all our high-quality books, call toll free 1-800-542-2595 or fax 1-877-542-2596.

Library of Congress Cataloging-in-Publication Data

Names: Rajczak Nelson, Kristen, author.
Title: Let's go strawberry picking / Kristen Rajczak Nelson.
Description: Buffalo, New York : Gareth Stevens Publishing, [2025] |
    Series: Let's have fun outside! | Includes index.
Identifiers: LCCN 2023045482 | ISBN 9781538294963 (library binding) | ISBN
    9781538294956 (paperback) | ISBN 9781538294970 (ebook)
Subjects: LCSH: Strawberries–Juvenile literature. |
    Strawberries–Harvesting–Juvenile literature. | Berries–Juvenile
    literature. | Berries–Harvesting–Juvenile literature.
Classification: LCC SB385 .R35 2025 | DDC 634/.75–dc23/eng/20231106
LC record available at https://lccn.loc.gov/2023045482

Published in 2025 by
Gareth Stevens Publishing
2544 Clinton Street
Buffalo, NY 14224

Copyright © 2025 Gareth Stevens Publishing

Designer: Claire Zimmermann
Editor: Kristen Nelson

Photo credits: Cover, p. 1 Irina Wilhauk/Shutterstock.com; pp. 5, 24 (middle) Tiplyashina Evgeniya/Shutterstock.com; p. 7 San Fran Love/Shutterstock.com; pp. 9, 24 (right) barmalini/Shutterstock.com; p. 11 hlphoto/Shutterstock.com; p. 13 SewCreamStudio/Shutterstock.com; pp. 15, 17, 24 (left) Shestakoff/Shutterstock.com; p. 19 Alexandra Preston/Shutterstock.com; p. 21 ajlatan/Shutterstock.com; p. 23 Likee68/Shutterstock.com.

Printed in the United States of America

Some of the images in this book illustrate individuals who are models. The depictions do not imply actual situations or events.

CPSIA compliance information: Batch #CSGS25: For further information contact Gareth Stevens, at 1-800-542-2595.

Find us on

Contents

The sun is sunny
and warm.
Let's go
strawberry picking!

We go to the farm. Strawberries grow there!

Strawberry plants grow white flowers.
Then green fruits grow.

They get bigger.
They turn white.
They turn red!

We each have a basket.
We look for red berries.
We pull berries off
the plant.

I fill my basket!

I taste a berry too.
Auntie tells us
to wait for more!

The farmer weighs our berries.
We pay for them.

Auntie washes
the berries.
We eat them for a snack!

Let's pick
blueberries next!

23

Words to Know

basket   strawberry   flower

Index